MUSINGS

H. Nelson Fitton

Order this book online at www.trafford.com
or email orders@trafford.com

Most Trafford titles are also available at major online book retailers.

Printed in Victoria, BC, Canada.

ISBN: 978-1-4269-2212-1

*Our mission is to efficiently provide the world's finest, most comprehensive book publishing
service, enabling every author to experience success. To find out how to publish your book, your
way, and have it available worldwide, visit us online at www.trafford.com*

Trafford rev. 11/20/2009

www.trafford.com

North America & international
toll-free: 1 888 232 4444 (USA & Canada)
phone: 250 383 6864 ♦ fax: 812 355 4082

"Creation seemed a mighty crack
To make me visible."

Emily Dickinson

My deep appreciation goes to
my wife, Judy, whose indispensable
help made this book possible.

CONTENTS

I. POEMS

ABSENCE

You were in my thoughts,
Warmly, vividly, obsessively,
And I kept wanting to touch you,
To look into your eyes,
To embrace you, to kiss you,
And kiss you, and kiss you.
I kept seeing you
And holding you in my thoughts,
Not able to touch you
Or feel your softness
Or speak softly to you.
Oh how my arms ached to hold you,
Tight and tighter,
As tightly as I could
To never let you escape again.
Now you are back
And I can hold you
Not just in my thoughts
But fully in my embracing arms
That informs me
How desperately I missed you.

ALL GOD'S CHILDREN

Some players,
Those warriors of the football field,
Fall on their knees,
After they score,
In a tense football game.
And some cross themselves with thanks
For their accomplishments.
But who are they thanking?
The almighty?
God doesn't take sides,
He gives free will
For players to crash into each other,
And He's surely sad
To see injuries,
And I'm sure He loves to hear prayers,
But they don't make Him favor
One side or the other--
No winning or losing
By His hand.
Win or lose,
It all has to do with skill
And determination,
Maybe a little luck,
As God watches nonpartisan--
All are God's children
On both sides of the ball.

ALL GOLDEN DAYS
(to Bernice after Fifty Years)

The years that grant the time
For love to reach its grandest heights
Have given us a most precious gift--
This year of gold, this year of lights.

What a lovely garden we have made,
And you have been the sun to give it life.
Not more than now can the flowers bear,
Not more than now have their sweetness filled the air.

Yes, fifty years have made their golden way
And the fresh faces of our youth are past.
Yet youthful passion glows anew each day
To make a mockery of time's conquests.

Time does not diminish the longing
For the gentle word, the tender touch,
The radiant smile, the warm embrace
That give meaning to all things around us.

This golden year is but the sum
That frames the past, all golden days.
Hand in hand we'll journey as before
To new days, all golden to the end of time.

ALZHEIMER'S
(for Mary Ruth Oldt French, M.D.)

No more will the landscape of the cell
And the caverns of flesh and bone
Reveal to her searching eye
The enemies that ravage body and mind.

No more will the light of science
Beam from her caring heart
To brighten her way in the healing art
In a calling loved and duty bound.

Now shadows fill this once bright mind
And a stark repose has stilled her lively face.
Yet a generous smile beams through the mask,
Glowing from a heart that nurtured family and friends.

What triumph is there for this treachery
Of robbing the memory of its treasured past,
And of taking away the happy hours
Of days so bright and strongly cast?

Those she touched still feel the glow
Of a fulfilling past so presently felt.
No darkness can fall upon her life,
And that is where the triumph lies.

ANGELS

We speak of angels,
But few believe
They exist.
Most relegate them
To a fairyland.
The Bible rescues their existence
And their place in life,
As the believers hang on to the thought
That the angels
Will show up one day
To rescue us.

AT GLEN ECHO PARK

Riding up and down on a wooden horse
Moving in a circular course,
Going 'round and 'round
To music with a tinny sound,
A sound almost hypnotic
As we approached the amusement park.
Now to ride that wooden horse again.
As my wife implored, after so many years it's been,
Such a silly notion I couldn't bear
And be the object of many stares.
So to ride that silly horse I wouldn't dare,
For after all, I wasn't a kid anymore,
And besmirch my dignity there.
It would take a stiff drink, or two or three,
To break my will you see,
Or to fall under someone's spell.
And that is where my will broke down
A talent for which my wife's renowned,
So it wasn't the drink, but my wife's usual spell.
Yes, I got to ride that infernal horse—
Oh well.

BEAUTY'S SEDUCTION

Should I let beauty steal my eye
And influence my heart to comply?
Passion should follow reason
In life and love in every season.

BEAUTY'S SPELL
(Imitating Early Romantic Poets)

My eyes gaze with delight
When she comes in my sight.
And then when she doth flee
A vision of her constantly visits me.

There's a garden in her face
That all its lush beauties embrace.
Her sunlight beauty shines so fair
Graced softly with her lovely hair.

She is so gentle and rich in lovely parts
With all her charm and graceful arts.
Her springtime of youth shall never fade
For she is so wonderfully made.

All her acts make such joys
Other pleasures are but toys.
And if she frowns upon my ways
It clouds my days.

She is indeed so very gay
And is a joy in every way.
Her beauty bring eternal quest
For her love in many a man's breast.

Is there a man so true
Who wouldn't her faith undo?
But she must not forever doubt
And let love's fire go out.

Never should she love unless she can
Bear up to the faults of men.
They may well bring her discontent
But her charm will bring repent.

Will she bear with me my sins of clay?
For I too, can stumble on the way.
But if I give her any pain
Despair would fall on me like rain.

For she alone can pleasure lift
And send my heavy gloom adrift.
If she turns from me her lovely smile
I would wither in a while.

BECAUSE YOU WERE THERE
(for Anne Renninger)

Each time we met to prepare
To make our talents blend in song and dance,
We reached across the past
To rescue what once was there.

Our youthful hopes were long gone
And so our talents seemed forever lost to time.
But now as with the birdsongs of spring
The melodies of our spring have returned reborn.

The glorious song sounds from piano and voice,
And from the taps our feet produced
Came in grand renewal
For our hearts to rejoice.

Only from the heart does music come,
To find its way out from our long lost past
For us to reclaim,
And it could have only happened because you were there.

BIRDSONGS

I enter into nature's chamber of birdsongs,
The sounds seemingly random,
And not from a choir.
Yet the blend of notes is so rhythmically sweet
There must be a choirmaster there, somewhere,
To shape the melodies from center stage.
I need not see a stage
Or see a choir.
So let the songs fill the air
With melodious birdsongs
To delight our ears,
And somewhere there is a choirmaster
Behind it all,
And since the sounds are heavenly,
I look to the heavens
And wonder if the choirmaster is there.

BODY LANGUAGE

Some things anatomical
Can be absolutely comical
When the parts so digress
At the time of undress.

BOOKS, BOOKS, BOOKS

I'm surrounded by books, books, books
And more books,
Jammed on shelves groaning from overload
And spread about in various rooms
On chairs, tables, and the floor
With little space left and lusting for more.
What wonders there are in this enchantment of excess
From which I glean so many delights
At any hour, day, or night.
Knowledge, wisdom, great literature, poetry,
And infinitely more,
Stand ready to feed my bookish voracious appetite
Nourished by this plentitude.
Yet if I encounter another used book store
I'll deftly find space for more
Knowing that through books
There are more worlds to conquer,
And explore.

BRAGGART

If in your social intercourse
You tend to exaggerate your every skill and deed,
Do so with a skilled straight face
And with deceiving grace,
Or you'll not succeed.
Some people deem this a form of lying,
Particularly in the self aggrandizing,
And that day will come
When you lose the art
And your deception
Will come apart.
So when you fear you might be caught
And you get terribly overwrought,
It's time for you to retreat
And spare you listeners further grief.

THE CHALLENGE

What can we do
To establish a culture
of smiles,
of laughter,
of joy,
To overcome the entrenched pessimism
That overwhelms us daily
By harsh reality?
All things have seemed to come apart:
Wars continue and spread,
Rains flood homes and towns,
Fires scar the land,
As nature deals with a heavy hand,
And the economy falls into a bottomless pit,
Leaving families adrift with no job, no home,
Making a fiction of
I'm alright, you're alright,
Hopelessness abounds.
So we need what can bond us,
And look for things that bring delight
Rather than fright.
Start smiling, laughing, finding joy
And finding new wings to fly;
In the meantime,
I'm laughing,
And I don't know why.

CHELSEA

Chelsea was a charismatic golden lab
Full of mischief, but saintly, too.
And in her loving ways as a companion,
Crafty and smart, matched by few.

When she was naughty she knew it was so,
Then try to make amends
And then wait for my hug
As she further nourished our love.

She mourned for my wife for a long time to come
And in uncanny ways she knew of my hurt
And lifted my spirit
As nothing else could.

She would wake me each morning
By slapping on my bed,
And if ignored by that tactic
She would slap even harder.

She watched my eyes
And as soon as they opened
Her tail would wag furiously
Not missing a beat.

She would charge down the stairs
To begin the day with run and meal
And then fill the day
With her presence.

She always wanted to be at my side,
So whenever I returned home after a chore
She was always waiting at the door
Wagging her tail with appropriate barking.

Her supreme achievement came one day
When I found her roaming on the roof of the house
After much coaxing she came down
Barking proudly for her feat.

I have her picture hanging proudly in my den
With mischief gleaming in her eyes
Still ready to outwit me
As she always did—with charm.

DAD'S HIDDEN AGENDA

One day when I went walking with my father,
who was a fast walker,
And I was nearly 12
And felt I was beginning to grow up,
With my father pushing it.
He moved so fast
It felt beyond my endurance
And my short skinny legs
Too strained to keep up
With my breath running out.
I asked for a rest,
If just for a moment,
But his response to my pleas was "it's good for you,
Stick it out."
Time moved on and my legs grew long
And I stuck it out
As my father wished,
And through the years he kept up his fast pace.
But I wonder if these early walks
Had a hidden agenda--
To prepare me for years ahead for the track team
And my many triumphs.

DARK DAYS

It is said,
You have to be depressed
To be a true poet.
If that is so,
Is it because poets
Face up to reality
And reality is a demon
Full of despair and hopelessness,
And pain,
Poised to break your heart
And poison your spirit?
And that's only the beginning:
Throughout the world,
Unbounded in misery,
You are mercilessly confronted by
Poverty, starvation, disease,
Floods, hurricanes, terrorism, economic distress,
And the ubiquitous war,
Well entrenched from the past,
And so on.
Through this darkness of spirit
You can find little specks of light
Where joy can be found
In family, friends, love, and faith
With God lighting the way,
The challenge continues
With the poets.

A DEEP LOVE

I spawn dreams and fantasies
Of your face, your voice, your figure,
Your smile, your eloquent eyes.
I hear the music from your heart
That makes my heart sing.
I desperately reach out for you,
To embrace you warmly,
To kiss you passionately,
And to love you to its ultimate expression
That is known only in ecstasy.
But it cannot be
For fate has dealt its wicked blow
To tantalize me with what I cannot hope to have
And left me to my dreams and fantasies of you
To sustain my hungry heart.

DESPERATE SOLUTION

All too often I can't find my keys
When I should find them in a breeze.
And since I can't use my memory in reliable complicity
I wind up relying on serendipity.

DISAPPEARING ACT

They suddenly come to me
As a feast of words
For a poem.
But faster than I can grasp them
Many evade me, forever lost.
For what you don't seize instantly,
You lose irretrievably,
Painfully.
Where the words come from
I don't know,
But I do know the words can be precious
And with that loss
The poem suffers
As does the poet.

DIVINE CREATION

The beauty of the universe
Would be meaningless
If there were no people
To see the glory of God's creation.
Why would we have such beauty
Without the mind of people
And the molding of further beauty
By their hands to show
It was not all by chance
But by design?

DIXIE

In the South of Confederate heritage,
Among towns large and small,
Stand monuments to bravery
Of the men in gray,
In a war still being fought
In the hearts of southern ersatz patriots,
Never diminishing in time.
It would take another war
To get those monuments down.
Nor will the stirring sounds of Dixie,
A monument in itself,
Ever be muted,
And whenever the first notes are sounded,
The southern heart beats in a rousing spirit
Even though the song was composed
By a Yankee from New York.
Great irony arose from southern ashes
When northern industry moved en masse south
For its rebirth,
As the monuments endure,
And the sound of Dixie
Still beats in the southern heart.

DREAM WORLD

As my eyes grow heavy in the night,
I love the moonlight
That beams its soft rays
Into my subconscious realm
Where delightful fantasies
Unfold.
My world is then a dream world
Like whispers barely heard,
And secret thoughts
Are born deep inside
Detached from a frenzied world.
Unencumbered, the soft rays
Hold dominance
In a hypnotic way
To produce poetic verse
That comes from heaven knows where.

ECHOES OF THE YEAR

As a dedicated hoofer and warbler
And most of all a poet
Always looking for rhymes to sing,
I scan the closing year as a treasured time
For the melodic pleasures it gave my ear.
I still hear the music, taps, and rhymes,
They endure in my mind
Like echoes from the year
To give me double pleasure.
And as the year folds into the past,
There comes the thrill of anticipation
Of new rhymes and new sounds
For new echoes.

EITHER WAY

How many important things
Are left unsaid,
And how many things
Not important are said?
It doesn't matter in the long run
For one word has found the truth in both—
Love.

THE ELOQUENCE OF SILENCE

A special person,
A special place,
And an unbroken silence.
We do not break it then,
When deep love needs no words—
Only the silent echoes,
Of all we have spoken,
Of all we have felt,
And all we have done together.
Our silence is sweet and the echoes eloquent
Anything else diminishes them.

ENCHANTED DAYS

I went by my old school yard in a fit of nostalgia
And many scenes scrambled through the haze of my memory
Clearing into sights and sounds of those enchanting days
That revealed before me the breathing sight
Of my grade school friends,
Of the seeming chaos of activity
Yet always under the teacher's control.

Yes, the playground I saw so clearly was empty,
But I saw it filled with so many familiar faces in every detail
Amidst the pushing and shoving and running
Produced by all those recess dynamos.
And I could hear the high decibel babble above the din of traffic
Intruding on my fantasy.

And there was the prettiest girl, my secret love,
With her neat curls and pristine image,
Just as she was then.
I then wondered if all this enchantment of my childhood
Was as it really was or reshaped the sugarcoated,
Nothing negative allowed.

It doesn't matter, for I shall hold on to that enchanted place,
Even if I was fooling myself
As I left that empty school yard
Wishing it was all retrievable.

THE END OF THE RAINBOW

What one won't try to do to find the pot of gold
At the end of the rainbow.
Those who lay their bets at the casino table
Think the luck of the spin or the draw of the cards
Will reach to the pot
At the end of the rainbow.
And worse are those who squander money they can't afford,
Week after week,
As they fall for the lure of the lottery.
Government agencies with their hard sell
Readily find their victims across the land,
Sucking up their hard earned money,
Appealing to their greed
With limitless largesse unearned,
Officially sanctioned as though morally correct,
While again and again ad infinitim
The countless victims don't win,
As the habit grows with eternal hope.
When, oh when, will the victims learn
It's all a hidden tax,
That they eagerly pay and often can ill afford.
And when, oh when will they learn
There is no pot of gold at the end of the rainbow?
There isn't even a rainbow—
But the government commercials won't tell you so.

ENDURING FAITH

So many times, countless they are,
Have I approached with wonder that graceful image
Called the Old Presbyterian Meeting House,
In the grand Old Town of Alexandria, Virginia.
So many times, each time a blessing,
Have I entered that sanctuary of divine dignity
That made each visit an act of faith.
So many times in that holy place
Have I fought off doubts
With thoughts, strength, and zeal.
So many times have I felt the vibrancy
From the pulpit and the pews
And feeling and hearing the Gospel
As a fortress against all things evil
And so many times have I heard
The silence of all prayers said there
Fulfilled in their faithful legacy;
It all shall be so
In the future.

ENTROPY

Broken bodies,
Broken minds,
Broken hearts,
Sight and hearing in fast decline.

Broken hopes,
Broken dreams,
Shattered desires,
None to be redeemed.

Shattered families,
Shattered friendship ties,
Fun and frolic now gone,
once in great supply.

Now melancholy fills the faces,
Where smiles once beamed,
And loneliness fills the air
Where tears now stream.

The world still turns
But not for them, you see,
For there is no future
But to live in ignominy--
Nursing home.

EROTIC LARGESSE

The crop is ripe out there men,
Your lust can be served,
You won't have to work so hard,
The girls are ready to oblige.
This is your golden age for bedding,
So what more could you want
From such easy pickings?
Just think, no responsibilities,
No commitment necessary,
Just be ready for the next one,
This bounty of delight.
Your male counterparts of an earlier time
Never could have expected such erotic largesse,
Like being let loose in a candy factory;
But all delights come with a price,
Here venereal disease will follow you around
Now abundant.
Also, some day you'll want a bride
And you must pick from the same pickings,
So what will you have to offer in the picking.
Good luck men.

FATE

Fate is always with us
Poised to strike
With wind, water, fire,
Volcano, earthquake,
Or any other force of nature,
Uncontrollable,
Producing the ultimate
In pain and suffering,
Demolishing homes, and serenity,
And destroying a lifetime of treasures,
Impossible to replace,
Cruelly wiped out,
Wiped out,
Total destruction,
No way to have prevented it,
No way to fight it,
Helpless,
In fate's crushing grip,
And devastating to see and feel.
But life must go on,
Whatever the loss, whatever the hurt,
For in the end it's fortitude that prevails,
Knowing you will rise again.

FIDELITY

Many lovely women pass by,
But only one can fill my eye.
You are the only one I see,
And that's the way it will always be.

A FIELD OF DAISIES

I came upon a field of daisies
With their radiant faces
Rising, proud among wild grasses.
Spread and clustered as nature deemed
They swayed with the gentle breeze
As gracefully as ballet dancers.
Almost ghostly at first sight
Appeared a solitary figure
That stirred my thoughts of a distant past,
I saw a young lady with flowing hair
And a softness as out of a long lost dream
Gathering her bouquet with gentle care.
There was my mother, a vision I couldn't suppress,
Who on our many summer drives
Gathered her harvest from a field's largess.
Seized, as I was, by this sudden memory,
That young lady and my mother
Were one in my fantasy.
Yes, it wasn't really my mother I saw,
Still I heard her whisper to me,
Why don't people pick daisies any more?
I know my fantasy will remain
Each summer when the daisies bloom
And I shall pass that way again.

THE FLAME STILL BURNS
(for Judy)

The heart beats faster and the mind goes spinning
To a higher level of feeling, emotion, warmth, intensity,
When that heart joins another heart
In a new world of hope, commitment, and deep affection.
When that reaches into the lives of older people,
Love is rekindled
And youthful passions can grow anew
And need not fade nor become shallow.
And, too, all things around take a new meaning
As new challenges will abound.
The reach for bliss will also be there
As though youth has grown eternal.
But time and age will keep reality in focus,
And that is not a weight too heavy to carry.
The path is there for us to travel
Hand in hand--
Still the flame burns.

FLOWERS PLUCKED TOO SOON

The canons have thrust their fusillade
And the snapping sounds of rifles have abated
After dispatching their lethal messages.
Bodies, still strewn in their grotesques forms,
Profane the earth where once pristine fields
Flattered the eye to the far horizon.
Now a deathly silence falls heavy here
Upon a ghastly sight too often seen,
Repeated ceaselessly from ancient times.
In the silence of this numbing sight,
We can hear the pleading echoes across time:
Why? We were all of us flowers plucked too soon.

FOR THE JOY THEY BRING

Still hoofing, still warbling,
And still looking for rhymes that sing.
And with my lovely spouse
I roam the beauties of the land
Usually to the hills
Rather than to the water and sand.
So I send out words on the wing
With melodies for the ear
And for the joy they bring.

GEORGE WASHINGTON'S HOMETOWN

I often roam the streets of Old Town,
Alexandria, Virginia,
At a place where the historic Potomac River flows,
And I never cease to yield to the spell
It casts in beauty and in fame.
The lovely homes with their neat facades
Bathe in notable charm,
Time tested authentic,
Looking much as they did
When George Washington rode into town
From nearby Mount Vernon.
And as I roam the streets
I feel the pulse of Old Town's history
As the past merges with the present
To make me feel I was there
Sharing in the riches that history made.
I see George Washington mounting his horse
And a call to his troops,
To go with him to fight a war,
And they did,
That would change the world.
Yes, as I roam the Old Town streets,
In that historic place along the Potomac,
I continue to see the beauty of the present
And the vibrancy of a glowing past.

GOALS

How often do we work for a goal
And we achieve it
Only to find nothing there,
As there is no pot of gold
At the end of the rainbow—
Unless you can find the end.

GOD'S LIGHT

In a quiet neighborhood
In Springfield, Virginia,
Stands Grace Presbyterian Church
With its graceful lines crowned by a steeple
Reaching up toward heaven
Producing an aura of divine dignity.
When you enter the sanctuary you cannot fail to feel
The vibrancy of a congregation
Deep in faith with open arms
Not confined there
But spread where poverty, hunger, and hopelessness abound.
They reach out from neighborhoods to foreign lands,
Honduras and the Middle East,
To name two
To show there are no limits in time and place
Where the heart provides.
Here is the power of just one giving church
To reach out to a broken world,
With a light of hope,
A light that makes a difference,
For it's God's light,
Yes,
It's God's light.

GROWING OLD

With youth long past,
The insults of time,
Felt keenly in silence,
Echo in shouts,
Not in whimpers.

HAIR SECRET

Oh how he flaunts his great head of hair
And keeps it groomed with the greatest of care.
But at bedtime when he's safely alone
That hair comes off, it's not his own.

HAPPY TIMES ON CAMPUS

It seems that going to college
Is a blatant waste of resources
With so many students ill prepared
And dominating their time
Partying, copulating, boozing, smoking pot,
Cheating on exams, and manipulating
Into easy courses.
To not hinder their present activities,
Let them major in basket weaving
And given an A
To keep the joys of the campus
Intact.

THE HARVEST OF THE YEARS
(to Lindalee and Bob on their Silver Wedding Anniversary)

The bequest of time that has tendered
The richness of your shining love
Abounds in this time when you have reached
The pure silver your twenty-five years have rendered.

The lovely days you have made together
And all the lovely times you have shared with others
Have forged a bond of love and strength
That can't be bounded by depth or width or length.

When your two hearts as destined came together
And found that richness the future would prove,
The patterns for your vibrant lives were cast
Where no goal was too far or challenge too vast.

And now those years to silver have past,
With your horizons furthered and course ever widened,
You've seen only the prelude, the beginning
With your gathering future still being cast.

Into that abounding future you will sail
The same steady course that in the past prevailed,
Filled with love and trust and sharing,
All done with your youthful zest and daring.

HE IS SUFFERING

He is suffering,
misery,
pain,
stress,
hurt,
distress,
despair,
anguish,
agony,
Joe just lost his job.

HER LAST SMILES
(for Bernice Fitton)

There in the bright light of day
And into the dark hours of the night,
Around the lumbering clock,
The weight of time grew as the hours ticked away.

It was in a place of desperate waiting,
In that place of the desperately ill,
Where no hope abided
Within the reach of modern healing.

Bernice quickly knew her fate when taken there
For the eloquence of death was all around,
With its unambiguous message
Sent in a grim finality unbound.

Yet there the dignity of life held firm
Against death's artless pursuit,
Where skilled hands quelled relentless pain
And let waning life pass in soft peace.

And so with Bernice the last hours softly passed
Inevitably to reach that final hour,
Ending a vigil of love among family and friends,
A love that held all things together.

And those she touched still see the glow
That beamed from her radiant face,
And her smiles held true, her great triumph,
At that Hospice till the end.

HIDDEN TAX

The lottery is a crafty ruse
Where a few win and most always lose.
And among those who take the hit
Are so many who can hardly afford it,
Yet the habit grows with eternal hope,
As the victims continue on this slippery slope.
And each plays this game the governments back
And don't reveal that it's a hidden tax.
For those who do not play this game,
This tax under another name,
Are quite happy to let the victims feed
This loser's game of eternal greed.

HONEYSUCKLE

Viewed from my back porch
My discerning eye beholds
A long stretch of honeysuckle
Robustly announcing Spring has come.

Like a wall it stretches,
Wild, uncontrolled, and lush
Firmly grasping to an old fence
Coming from an earlier time.

Uninterrupted in its pursuit of space,
No gaps in the wall, no competing bushes,
The vine rises tall and firm
As nature commands.

There is a kind of beauty about it
With its sweet smelling blossoms,
I would not want to give it a manicure,
This thicket that makes a wall.

It shuts off neighbor from neighbor,
More so as the years mount up,
Still we'll not disturb this barrier
But let nature take its course.

Yes, we seldom visit each other
But we're good neighbors just the same.
So what seems to divide us
Keeps us friends more than in name.

HOPE
(for Bernice)

As she battles the rigors of lethal cancer,
I have searched for any signs of hope,
Beyond the limits of medicine's scope,
To give comfort to her and to me.
We have drawn upon our faith and inner strength,
Yet feel the gripping challenge there
That such uncertainty begets.
But there among her lovely azaleas,
She so adores and has so lovingly nurtured,
One bush full of blossoms in full radiance
In the forbidden unseason of August,
Crying out as if to say:
Bernice, I send you a message from us all
That we love you for all your tender care
And that you let my special garment be
A message of hope and love—
A message that of this kind we cannot dare
Without our gift being from the hand of God.

HUMMINGBIRDS
(A Reflection of Mom)

I thought of you with each mounting chore
And wondered how you could do more,
Yet somehow it all seems to fit your style,
Always moving with a broad smile.
Then I sought a word to portray
How you did it day after day.
Then I found the exact word to fit
By never seeming to tire one bit:
You are an indefatigable hummingbird,
Which brought me to how much I do
And realize I'm a hummingbird too.

I HEAR WEDDING BELLS
(for Judy)

I hear the sound of wedding bells
Ringing out joyously what they tell.
Many members of family and special friends
Packed with love in a grand room
That lifts the heart and dazzles the eye.
I hear the sound of wedding bells
Ringing out for the appearance of the wedding dress
For the bride to glow in,
And the radiance of her smile
To light up the audience, friend and kin.
I hear the sound of wedding bells
Ringing out for the ceremony
And I hear the mellifluous voice
Of the minister as he joins the two as one
With the ring that will light up the days to come.
I hear the sound of wedding bells
With greater intensity, for I am to be joined at her side.

I LOVE YOU

I love you
Not only because I will it.
I love you because all things tell me to.
In music, I hear the melody of your voice.
In the flowers, I see your gentleness
And smell your fragrance.
In the breeze, I feel your soft breath.
In the relentless waves of the ocean,
I hear your name over and over.
In everything soft I touch, I feel your hand.
I look at other faces and all are blank,
And I fill in yours.
Everything around me is infused with your spirit.
My pillow always waits for your soft hair
To settle against my face.
I do not think of you with unbridled passions
That masquerade as love.
I think of you with purity of your whole being,
And as all things tell me to.

I PROMISE

I will build her a house
With a determined will
And calloused hands.
I will make her a princess,
And the house will be a palace.
I will watch over her
And protect her from harm.
I will worry about her when she is ill,
And I will be anxious when we are apart.
No day will be dull,
Because I will make each day a surprise.
I will love her as the waves love the shore:
Constantly,
Sometimes gently,
Sometimes vigorously,
Always passionately,
As gifts of providence.
She will always be in my embrace,
Whether near or far.

I SING A LULLABY

I sing a lullaby, soft and gentle,
To all those babies wrenched from wombs,
Never to know love, but only death
Before their blessed birth.

I sing a lullaby to make them live
In my thoughts and aching heart,
A lullaby they will never hear
With a delighted ear.

And I sing a lullaby
To honor them in their sacrifice
To acts of brief pleasures and thrills,
The finality in the name of choice.

If only the mothers with warm hearts
Had made the choice for life not death
And sung their lovely lullabies
To those sweet smiling faces.

I THINK I SHALL TELL YOU
(to Bernice)

When our love was new
Fresh and sweet,
And we had parted for the day,
We had to phone each other,
Like impatient teenagers
Looking for anything to say.
Each evening at our embrace
I'd look upon your lovely face
Just like love at first sight.
Now so many years are gone
With passion tamed, but still so strong,
Do you know how much you are in my thoughts,
Wherever you are, far or near,
Beyond my sight, beyond my ear?
That's the way it's always been,
Now as much as it was then.
I think I shall tell you
The way I did before.

IT ALL MATTERS

Entropy makes us all the same
At the end.
But getting there is a whole different story
Where fate and failure travel as one
While another is bathed in glory.
Does it matter that one succeeds
And another fails?
Does it matter that one dies young
While another does not?
Does it matter that one is fragile
While another is robust?
Does it matter that one lives a loving life
While another finds eternal strife?
Does it matter that one finds a healing faith
While another finds a life to scorn?
Yes, it all matters that life is not neatly packaged;
So we must accept what is given
And that starts with the strength of faith.

IT'S NOT PRUDITY

I don't condemn nudity
Because of any prudity,
It's that so many uninhibited
Are not that well distributed.

A KISS

Soft on the lips,
A kiss,
The passion of tender feelings
And joined delight,
No slobbering,
No snorting,
No biting,
Only pressing,
Until the thrill
Reaches its peak
For the next kiss
To be yearned for all the more.
Those who love
And feel the thrill,
That fullness of the lips fulfilled,
Know that the kiss
Not too short to reach its peak,
Not so long as to benumb the lips
Will reach for that ecstasy
That the well measured kiss
On the well chosen lips
Will yield.

THE LAST TO GO

Pity the poor man
Whose age keeps stretching out
Across time
Into his tottering years
With his longevity
Out pacing family and friends
While he survives alone,
Terribly alone,
To carry the heavy load of loneliness,
The last of the breed.
All whom he cherished,
All whom he loved
Remain only in memory,
A poor substitute
For what is lost.
This blessing of longevity,
The goal of most,
Can come at a high price
For the last to go.
So many he has mourned,
So many tears he has shed,
But no one is left
To mourn for him--
He's the last to go.

A LEGACY OF LOVE
(for Anita Owen)

On that date of loss when thoughts reached to the past
To summon up things to hold in treasure,
Anita's glowing light on us was cast
And her lasting love bequeathed beyond mortal measure.

Now that memories flood in and take root,
We still see her smile from that distant shore
And hear her soft voice that will never fall mute,
Giving us her embracing comfort as before.

She needed no heraldic crown to adorn her head
To give symbol to her special place.
She filled her many roles in life
That gleamed more than a crown by her noble grace.

As she reaches us across stretching time
All knowing her as a wife, a mother, a friend,
We know the legacy she has left us
Will remain with us, will know no end.

LET DOWN

When we hear from Doctor Ruth,
We expect to hear the sexual truth.
So it's super to know it's her credo
For us to flaunt our libido.
That makes us yearn for more advice
On finding our sexual paradise;
But then lost in her falsetto accent,
We have despaired over what she meant.

A LIFE TAKEN TOO SOON
(for Wilbur Fitton)

His was a life taken too soon
When all his misdeeds were behind him
And a future was filled with hope
Like a sunrise after the darkness of night.
His goodness had always been there,
There at the core,
But he struggled for identity and confidence
To find a firm direction.
Like an epiphany,
His world changed
As he pulled himself out of a morass
Of doubt and indecision,
To heights he knew not before
With his mind set for more education and a career
In criminal justice.
He thrust himself into his new direction
Full of energy and hope
Auguring that all was going well
Until a mortal blow
Shattered his hope of a promising future
Balefully contained in a single word—
Polio.
His helpless body, struggling for breath,
Was placed in an iron lung
That groaned with a foreboding cadence
Telling us that his hope filled future was ending.
Yet through it all his smiles prevailed
And his spirit kept high,
But the iron lung and his indomitable spirit
Were not enough,
For he died in three days at twenty four.
That was a life anew,
Budding—
A life taken much too soon.
And in less than a year
Polio was conquered.

LOOK AND LISTEN

Listen to the breezes,
It whispers it.
Listen to the ocean waves,
They shout it.
Listen to the birds,
They sing it.
Look at the moon,
It glows it.
Look at the stars,
They twinkle it.
And listen and look at me—
I love you.

LOST YOUTH

We often think youth is everything
And aging has a deadly sting.
But if that thought makes you antsy,
Just remember, youth is but a passing fancy.

LOTTERY'S TROUGH

They come hustling to the trough,
Like hogs salivating for swill,
Only to find the trough is bare
And the hope of easy wealth is not there.

That is the lottery, luring hordes to its trough
Empty to all but those luck has anointed,
To take all, leaving all others disappointed
Wallowing in the broken dreams of easy street.

The spasm of desire, intense and compelling,
For a fortune not earned, no labor spent,
Breeds illusions among the easy prey,
Who keep taking that path to the empty trough.

What crafty ruse the government spins
To draw the victims to that illusory win,
Chasing after an obscenely inflated sum,
And from so many inveterate losers, it comes.

But with official sanction, it seems so pure,
Even with so many victims they lure,
These victims who make it all succeed,
This money machine, this hidden tax fed by greed.

LOVE'S PROMISE
(to Bernice)

I shall love you
Even when my palsied hand
Reaches out desperately
In my last hours
To touch you once more
With the same tenderness
The steady hand knew before.

I shall love you
Even when my eyes grow dim
And darkness falls.
It shall be the same
As when your lovely face
Dazzled my youthful eyes
Full of light.

I shall grasp for your image
Though my mind fades
Into a misty retreat.
You shall be my last and sweetest memory,
Lighting up the darkness
As it descends.

MALE NEMESIS

There is a gland called prostate
That we men can come to hate.
When in our youth it gives us glee
For what it's meant to be.
But then we have only to wait
To suffer the consequences when it inflates.

THE MANY PARTS OF LOVE

Where has love gone,
That deep enduring dedication,
In this age of cynicism?
We still hunger for what heaven has deemed:
Two persons each unique,
Yet two spirits as one,
Two bodies as one,
With the warmth, the full offerings of each,
Where there are no secret dark corners,
Where there are no recesses
That cannot be reached,
Where their bodies are wondrous maps
To be explored as the miracles they are,
Where there are warm embraces
And tender searching hands,
All to be joyously given and received.
And all the words, and even silences,
Reach the heart and endure.
These measure not only the depth of love,
But its very essence.

MEMORIES OF JOY

Do not take away my childhood dreams,
For they were full of fun, games,
and giggly laughter,
And do not take away my grammar school thrills
Competing in sports in the school yard,
and discovering girls,
And do not take away the joy of the high school years,
and scoring high on exams,
And do not take away those heady days of college,
with their challenges in the sweat of learning,
And do not take away the loveliness of two wives,
one that left us much too soon,
And do not take away the years of toil,
reaching for the stars with failures and successes,
the latter dominating,
And do not take away my senior years
and my survival filled with writing poetry,
And do not take away the joy that will come with hope,
As I count my many blessings
And when I can still smile often and laugh heartily
And as I examine my past with its glowing joys,
I realize:
Someone up there was with me
All the way.

THE MIGHTY PEN

Writing with the pen, might in its past,
Flowing liquidly with grace,
Making the squiggles that form the words,
Is a sensual act joined lovingly with silent sounds,
With a message, simple or profound.
With technology's triumph, the tickling of the keys
Bring wonders to the page,
In neatly formed letters,
First on a wondrous screen,
So beckoning to one's anticipation.
Yet the pen does not dismay,
For it has locked into history
The passions of heart and mind,
Through bold and delicate times,
When eloquence flowed from the pen.
And though in the grip of the machine
Words find their cherished places,
Where but in the pen
Can the most personal feelings
Find their best way to the heart?

A MIRACLE

The sun sinks into the sea,
Without getting wet,
And it settles into the earth
As gracefully as a feather
Falling to the ground.
The illusion tells you
That when the sun
Rises from the sea
And from the earth
From the other side
To fool the eye
We need only to know
That behind the illusion
Is a miracle.

THE MIRROR'S CRIME

When you see the days and years compile
And your radiant youth is long erstwhile,
And when you think time's a curse,
And each day you think your wrinkles are worse;
And then you complain that life's not fair
When you think your face needs much repair,
Now you view your mirror as your enemy
That brazenly insults your anatomy,
There is nothing that could be clearer,
It's time for you to get a new mirror.

MISFITS

Noses come in great variety
Displayed in a prominent place.
And in our self-conscious society
Many feel their nose doesn't fit their face.

MODERN EDUCATION

See the college campuses
Teeming with fresh faced students
Eager to conquer the world
With knowledge gained from professors
Eager to share their knowledge and wisdom
In shaping pliable minds,
All done in a solemn vow.
What a pretty picture that makes
Of an educational triumph
To seal the future
With grand hopes.
Perhaps it was all a grand illusion
Now superseded by a new modernism
Full of freewill
Misdirected as education.
Where is the teaching
And where is the learning
Amidst dominating non curricula activities?
Not in the distractions of copulating,
Drinking, smoking pot,
Cheating on exams, partying
And taking easy courses.
Many graduates can't write a clear sentence,
Spell correctly, read beyond the comics.
And in the depth of humiliating ignorance,
Their knowledge of history and government
Is barren.
With a head full of mush,
They now are ready.

MOST BEAUTIFUL LADY

The most beautiful lady I ever saw
I saw working in a cafeteria
On a dreary highway in Hungary
On the way to Budapest.
Her bright blue eyes, appealing nose,
And immaculate skin,
All combining with a radiant face full of youth,
Enhanced by her soft blonde hair
Flowing luxuriantly down to her shoulders
With a softness you wanted to feel
And run your fingers through.
Her formless drab clothes could not conceal
Her legs, masterpieces of shapely form,
Or that she moved with elegance,
Out of character in such a dreary place.
She spoke broken English, barely understandable,
In a soft melodic voice
Punctuated by a delicious smile
That made you want to smile with her,
Contagious as it was.
Yet there was something haunting
That was revealed through her strained gentle smile
Emanating a sense of forlornness hard to describe.
Perhaps it was from the depressing atmosphere
And from the heavy pall of constant fear
Cast by the USSR.
But there she was
Her beauty shining through it all
Wasted in a cafeteria on a road to Budapest,
A memorable experience for me—
It was as if it happened yesterday.

NIGHT AND DAY

I love the morning light
When everything is pristine bright
And the beauty of the land
Trumps the darkness of night.

But there is something to be said
For the darkness of the night
That can ignite the imagination
Into deeper insight.

It's always on the agenda
That day follows night;
It never changes from the plan,
It's always precise.

It gives me double joy
To have a day and a night,
As it was planned that way
By design insight.

It's a most profound circumstance
That it all worked out this way,
For it could only be by design
And not by chance, I'd say.

A NIGHT BEFORE CHRISTMAS

The silence of the snow falling
On Christmas eve
Envelops in full whiteness
A peaceful night ahead.
But stirring there somewhere
Are the promises heavily stacked
In flight,
A specter moving beyond
Sight and sound,
Except in the world of childish delights.
So this is the night of great expectations
When the children think
Morning will never come,
But in the glow of Christmas morning
The magic moment has come
As all things seem to come alive
When the children shriek with joy,
Confirming
All the awaited expectations
Have been fulfilled.

NIGHT'S RAPTURE

When you are curled in bed
Snugly beside me each glorious night,
Sleep would not be sealed
Until you heard the loveliest words
Our rich language can yield.
And my eager arms would prove each night,
With the words sweetly said,
That true love is achieved
Not by words alone
But by touch and deed,
And then the sweet dreams can come.

NOSE JOB

The nose protrudes in a prominent place
And few like the way it fits their face.
So when you see a nose to marvel at
You wonder if it's what a scalpel begat.

NOSTALGIA

I drive through an area where towering buildings dwell
And where a vast shopping mall
Spreads in urban blight
While countless homes add to the sprawl,
Hardly an aesthetic sight,
A land that once was lush with green
And proud with wild flowers
From God's benevolent hand.
But progress laid claim
In its voracious quest
To transpose the land in its losing battle--
That leaves us to our memories
Of this once peaceful land,
And it's in our remembrance
Where our joy lies.
But I keep asking myself:
Where have all the daisies gone?

NOT IN VAIN

Time informs her eyes
Of their failing light,
But good enough to see
Her ashen gray skin
Creeping across her face
And her faltering energy
In flight,
And beyond recovery.

Her thinning lips tightly drawn
Into a bitter slit
Replacing her once radiant smile
That illuminated her life
And the lives of family and friends.
Now where is the joy
She so well knew,
Now beyond hope?

All is lost in the past
And deadens her future,
Bitterness prevailing,
But there are deep pockets of memories
Waiting to be explored
With the same heart beating
That knew joy before
And now not done in vain.

NOT THE SAME

I went to visit my old neighborhood
With unbounding excitement,
Hoping to recapture those golden days
For so long had been lodged in my memory.

The images were not ghostly,
But vivid,
As my fantasies had fashioned
And kept the past alive.

I often saw their animated faces
So full of energy,
So full of spirit
So full of life.

And I heard their voices,
Loud and shrieking,
Competing with each other,
So real.

As I drove through the neighborhood
I saw it as it once was,
And I placed all the people in there,
By name.

As passionate thoughts flooded my brain,
Suddenly a pall came over me
Spoiling my memory:
It was all just a fantasy.

There is no bridge from the past now
And the houses now mere symbols.
I can't really conjure up the past.
And these wonderful faces, the voices, and images—
Gone.

NURSING HOME

I often saw her sitting so fragile,
Condemned by the court of time,
In that place of broken bodies and minds,
Where all that's left is the dimming past.

Only the routine needs would interrupt
The solemn silence brooding over her
And would break into her reveries
That mourned the family ties, now foreclosed.

I would see her lift her drooping head,
Her sweet face belying her sad eyes,
And slowly raise a groping hand
As if searching for someone not there.

No children, no grandchildren with other concerns,
Were ever there for her groping hand.
Not a kiss, not an embrace, not loving words
To ignite the waning light in that sweet face.

Now when I pass her empty room,
I mourn her and opportunities lost
To have comforted her as a new friend
And been there for her groping hand.

ON THE TURNPIKE

As I merged into the pack of roaring vehicles
On a raceway called a turnpike,
The spirit of speed seized me
As though I was on a desperate mission.

Keeping pace with zooming cars and rumbling trucks,
I knew there would be no languishing on a full day's drive,
Only the euphoria that speed can bring
On the way to a family reunion.

With thoughts ahead of loving embraces
And at a time of colors only fall can beget,
The joy of anticipation increased with every mile,
As though Heaven itself had blessed the trip.

Then suddenly, as if by magic,
A large black lab appeared
And bolted in front of me, struck,
And thrown back to the side of the road.

I could see no way to help the dog, now writhing in pain,
Nor could I see any good Samaritans behind
As the scene receded quickly behind me
And left me with a bitter memory.

Why, after so many years, that scene still haunts me,
I cannot fathom,
And why, why did that dog stray
To that fatal place on that day?

THE PARADE

We watch the parade
Of the many wonderful things
That fill our eyes and hearts
And thrill our senses.
And there go the people,
So many we know.
So many we love,
We shall never see again.
But when the parade ends,
We shall be there with them.
We shall be there with them.

PERSEVERANCE

Keep Sailing with hope
Though the wind is fierce
And may rip your sails
If you keep them aloft,
As the raging waves
Have you at their mercy,
Tossing you about,
In thundering, roaring sounds,
Through the pea soup atmosphere,
You may think you see a hint of light
At the shore,
But whether real
Or illusion,
Keep weathering the storm
In it's vicious pounding
To match it
With your faith
And relentless hope.

PIERCING THE NIGHT

Piercing the night, thick above,
I searched for the light
To dispel my gloom and find my way.
Still the starry sheet
Without the bright of the moon
Spoke in countless ways
What light means in stark darkness
As the little flashes from the stars
Seemed to get brighter the more I looked.

POEMS OF MINE

All those poems of mine,
Each created in a moment of time,
Through which I hastily limped,
Wait passionately to be carefully primped.
But desperately I see each grain of sand descend
And I wonder if I shall even visit them again
To primp them up and make them sing.

THE POET

I try to explain the mysteries of life
And I stammer.
I read the explanations from the scientists
And they tell me not enough with their facts.
I ponder the profundities of the philosophers
And their endless chain of words befuddle me.
You find answers only when an inner voice
Speaks to you
And makes you a poet.

THE POWER OF WORDS

The Power of Words
Show up best
In poetry.
For that power
Of the words
Use many devices
To pamper the ear
And the mind
And beckon
To be spoken
As well as to reach
For emotion.

PRAYER UNBOUNDING

Everybody prays
Whether it's called prayer
Or not:

No matter the culture,
No matter the tradition,

No matter silent,
No matter spoken,

No matter standing,
No matter sitting,

No matter alone,
No matter with others.

In all forms
Prayer is universal,
and penetrating,

In our minds,
And in our hearts.

It is the wellspring of faith,
Powerful,
Restoring our souls.

This tide of faith and yearning
That carries us in its spiritual grip,
Prayer shows a depth
We cannot fathom.

So whether we cry out for help
Or rise up in unbounding joy,
God is always there
To illuminate our lives
In prayer.

PRAYERS ARE NOT FOR CERTAINTY

Prayers are not for certainty,
They are for hope.
They help us plead our case
For action on a problem
We can't conquer.
The pleas can range from the frivolous
To the miraculous,
And they help us reach to the edge of hope
As we struggle to be rescued.
We may pray for a loved one dying,
Or for the outcome of a football game,
Or we may need help in a love affair.
The extent of life's suffering
Has no end,
And there are no guarantees,
No matter the intensity of our pleas—
But God is always listening.

THE QUEST

The search for friendship
Is an eternal quest,
Straining in a world of separateness.
Often the search for deep friendships
Slips past us
Because we are always on the run.
And what do we gain
When the fear of closeness is too great
And the relationship will likely bring pain.
Friendship doesn't flourish
When conditions are laid down
And honesty corrupted
When no help comes when we are down.
Nor will friendship survive
On artful blandishment
Nor on fiction and not on truth.
In this tainted world of much mistrust
Where trust is a casualty
And deception an art.
More true friendship is needed
From the heart.

REACHING UP

The cathedrals reach up as if to heaven
Impregnable with walls of marble and stone,
Like fortresses
To thwart sin and the enemies of faith.

The expanse of beauty and splendor
And the vaulted ceilings for prayers to soar
Give nourishment
To the promise of eternal life.

And, too, there are those modest meeting houses,
Gracefully simple, each with its pointed spire
Life a finger to heaven,
Stand pristine in their durable white.

Their sanctuaries filled with faces known,
Where kindred spirits abound
In piety,
Strong as the soaring cathedral walls.

Their prayers rise as though their ceiling soar,
Where nothing could separate them
From eternity
But the weight of doubt and disbelief.

THE RECKONING

When we grow old and fear we look like those
Who carry the years heavy on their faces,
We curse time in its cruel work.

The once beaming faces, smooth and uncrumpled,
Now caricatures of our younger selves,
Daily is confirmed by an uncompromising mirror.

The depth of shock graphically is sustained
By the breathless search for magical repair
In pursuit of ersatz youth.

The grim search leads to grim results,
For the fountain of youth still is not there,
But the mirror is, to remind us of time's insults.

All is not lost when time seems not our friend.
We have other boundaries to explore,
With some of youth's fire somewhere there.

So let us leap, leap to new and daring wonders,
Where time does not limit the longing
For the tender touch, the beaming smile, the warm embrace.

Although the mirror haunts us still,
There yet burns in us some of youth's fire
To take us as far as our passions will.

REQUIEM

So many I have known,
So many I have loved,
So many slipping away
Into my fading memory,
Now gone, gone, gone,
Fiercely gone,
Never to be replaced,
Never to see their faces,
Never to hear their voices,
Never to feel their presence,
Except as they live in my memory,
As though their names
Are chiseled in granite,
Enduring.

SECOND THOUGHTS

He molded thoughts
With tender care.
And this before
He'd never dare.

But like the waves
Upon the sea
That reach the shores
Relentlessly.

His words came forth
Oh so strong
For the one he cared
Right or wrong.

To let her know
Thoughts from his breast
Might go astray
He should have guessed.

Should he have gone
So far afield
And gone so deep
For thoughts to yield?

What should he do
With words that flow
And gush like geysers
From deep below?

SELF DESTRUCTION

It's not whether the Holy Bible is fiction,
Or fantasy,
Or a collection of fairytales,
For it has already proved itself
in many ways
Through its divine messages,
its powerful messengers,
its saints,
its inspiring words
All together overpowering.
So the question is:
Why doesn't everyone
Accept the pathway
To the divine truth?
The solution is there
Waiting, waiting,
As the world destroys itself.

SENIOR CITIZENS

Many think our sport is the rocking chair
When we reach the age of Medicare.
Many say we're not where it's at
When our muscles give way to fat.
Many say we're in times undertow
When our step has begun to slow.
Many say we're growing senile
When we talk of things erstwhile.
Many say the mirror doesn't lie
When we disdain those who quantify.
To us it's become perfectly clear
It's a fraud to measure age by year.
So, what many say just ain't true;
We're not facing our Waterloo.
Yet when all is said and done,
We say this to all and one:
While we do not favor our rocking chair,
We thank our stars for Medicare.

A SHINING FOREVER

Moving into old
Is where the body and mind go
To haunt us on the way
To the inevitable process.
And with each day more self-consciousness grows
As the body parts grow more and more inefficient,
But with the hope that modern medicine
Can delay the crumbling from head to toe.
As time lays waste to our powers,
We can summon our will to fight
Against the unbeatable odds,
And in time spread our wings of faith
Into the shining forever.

A SINGLE ROSE

She wanted only one yellow rose,
Spurning the traditional dozen,
To be fused tightly in memory
Of a special time,
Of a special place,
And of a special event.
This rose in its singularity,
Golden in the light,
Would be poised
In a special place
To catch the curious eye.
She made a beautiful bride
And will hold that rose bright in memory,
For that rose will remain
Golden in her memory
Pressed forever
In a well selected book.

SNAPPY TAPPERS' LOVE SONG

We're here for you with spirits high
To lift your heart and dazzle your eye.
We promise a show of lively beat,
All done with taps on magic feet,
And to you we lovingly impart
The Snappy Tappers' love song.
We're here for you and you
To show you what we do
And bring you to a high,
Our troupe will try or die.
So join us in some sprightly fun,
And that means you, all everyone.
We Snappy Tappers' come with delight,
Put our feet in happy flight,
And make this day for you more bright,
Our Snappy Tappers' love song,
Love song
Snappy Tappers' love song.

A SPECIAL BREED

Politicians are a special breed
Who succeed on money, less on deed.

They devote most of their time on re-election,
Leaving little time for serious reflection.

They go to Washington with burning ambition,
With noble causes soon to be in remission.

With their innocent air and boldest nerve,
It's really number one they serve.

When will the people finally get wise
And no longer accept deception and lies?

It's all in the game our leaders play,
The difference between truth and what they say.

But any guise is worth every perk;
It's not serving those for whom they work.

What we need are servants of trust,
Not of power they so fervently lust.

Then why don't I put my hat in the ring
And stop all this griping and loathing?

It's simply useless for me to try,
Because I'll not master the art of the lie.

SPREAD JOY

The stars are old,
The full moon bold,
The sun is brazenly bright
And gives us eternal light.
The robust wind
Drives the roaring waves in.
Thus to the stars, moon, sun, and wind,
They know no end.
But for life, it's terribly brief,
Robbing us of time, a ruthless thief.
So while life is short, speeding on the wings,
And not part of the realm of timeless things
Take love with whatever your span
And spread joy as vigorously as you can.

SUMMER DELIGHT

Blink, blink, blink,
Little lightening bug
Are you blinking for a hug
Or are you blinking for a mate
Or are you blinking for a date?
We know of your amorous ways
And how well your courting pays,
But whatever is your purpose
In blinking tonight
Your blinking makes a lovely sight.

SURPRISE

My taste for hamburgers came early,
Well before my teens,
And as with my youthful friends,
I never got enough.
That made anticipation for more
All the more joyful,
Part of the supreme treat
For that next tasty bite, the next feast.
It seemed to have always been that way
Until I got a shattering shock
That quickly alienated
My taste buds
For many years to come.
It was on a calm, peaceful, normal day,
A time of my impressionable youth,
I learned from my mother
That hamburger came from cows.
Horrors!
How could that be?
I couldn't suppress the tormenting thought:
Are we cannibals?
The memory of that shock has never left me.

SUSPICION

There is danger:
You are a lovely lady, married,
And he is a man, married,
Often alone together.
People will say
You are a lovely lady, married,
And he is a man, married,
Often alone together.
That's all they need to think
And say,
There is the danger.

SWASHBUCKLING

When I was a youth of heroic dreams
And old enough to have discovered girls,
I saw Erol Flynn swashbuckling to fame
That sent my life into another world.

My grand ambition was to fight raging fires
Or cure people in Dr. Kildare's style,
But the indomitable Flynn changed all that
With his sword and sardonic smile.

I eagerly awaited each new adventure
To fill my new borne dreams
In the fashion of Walter Mitty,
But there was more of reality here then it seemed.

Off the silver screen burst dashing Flynn for real
With his amours rather than his blade to wield
To dally with some sweet young things,
Under age said the law.

But Flynn's conquests returned, a forceful thing,
With Flynn dominating my new dreams.
I wonder if there are any part-time jobs
In swashbuckling.

TAP DANCING DENTIST
(to Jack Sah)

At this dark time
Your light shines bright
To illuminate the lovely past you've made.

Your gentle voice with always a kind word to say
Will never stand mute, will never fade,
Its exuberance and wit in our hearts will stay.

All your many patients, the beneficiaries of your skill,
Knew that's where your heart was, too
Along with the forceps and drill.

You will remain in every room at home,
And there at the senior center you will be
And with the Snappy Tappers you still will roam.

Now the memories already abound
As we see your smile from that distant shore
We'll always know you are still around.

Jack, we can say by any measure
You left us a rich treasure—
And we will always remember.

THE TEST

With all the heavy baggage
We must carry through life,
How can we keep smiling?
With all the beauty of the land
And all the heartwarming relationships,
How can we not keep smiling?

THAT ONLY DREAMS CAN BRING

Like old picture long forgotten
Collecting dust in neglected drawers,
Or in a dark attic rich with stores,
There are dreams that fade into the past
Bound to youth that moves too fast.

And when your youth is gone
With those dreams that succumbed to an easier course
As you gave up or lost your way,
You can't go back
And retrieve those dreams for another day.

As with pictures long forgotten,
In those dark places of the past,
Why not brush off the dust the years accrued
And look again at the dreams you lost
Now with a new vision the years have taught?

Time gives out its own secrets,
That you'll find here:
That ambition, courage, and busy hands
Need a powerful direction that only dreams can bring.

THERE ARE NO GRAVES

There are no graves
For those torn from the womb,
With head and body shaped,
Fingers and toes formed,
A heart beating,
A nervous system that knows pain,
Persons never to see the wonders of the world,
Or experience the gifts of life,
Or give to life,
As future scientists, doctors, lawyers,
Engineers, world leaders, inventors,
Workers, artists, poets…,
Or feel the touch of another,
Or bathe in love's rapture,
Or live to give life and gifts of love
To future generations.
They know only the slaughter,
Their execution in an inhuman world
Where the silent screams of the helpless
Go unheeded,
Where the unprotected
Have no rights,
Where they are disenfranchised
For convenience
And have no hope of appeal.
Their gruesome fate is the garbage can,
Their ignominious cemetery.
There are no solemn services for them,
From the heartless, the brutal,
A breed of protected killers.
Their victims are the nameless—
Forever the nameless.
But the horror of the act
Does have a name—
Holocaust.
It's legally called choice,
Surely a choice in the work of the devil.
And there are no graves.

THIS WAS MEANT TO BE

What the past reveals
Can enrich the present in surprising ways,
And that the truth was sealed
When you were sent to me
By some angel
To assuage my pains of grief
And to bring light into my dark days.
That light has come through doors of delight
You have opened for me,
And somewhere I hear a voice that says:
"This was meant to be."

TIME UNRESTRAINED

We are tightly bound by oppressive time
That is always with us
Stealing our future
Like a thief committing a crime.

It's an ally of fate,
And its grip we can't escape,
And in the end it always wins,
Our loss irretrievable.

And then there is the insidious culprit entropy
Digging deep furrows in once a youthful face
To continue its lethal course
Beyond the hope of rescue in this deadly race.

So as we look with dread to a condemned future,
We try to hold back oppressive time
With potions, lotions, and creams
Culminating in our silent screams.

And with our lost youth and hopelessness,
Time is not benevolent in its final price,
Yet life is still precious enough
To pay the heavy price.

For all the past delights of family and friends
Still rest gently in sweet thoughts and memories,
And as we look up and across the vast expanse of heaven
All things final can be lighted with a loving smile.

TIME'S CURSE

When you see the days and years compile
And your radiant youth is long erstwhile,
And when you think time's a curse
And each day you think your wrinkles are worse,
And then you complain that life's not fair
When you think your face needs much repair,
You know then your mirror is your enemy
That brazenly insults your anatomy,
There is nothing that could be clearer,
It's time for you to get a new mirror.

TIME'S TREASURE

Your summer face
Will succumb to winter's wrath
And suffer disgrace
In time's ravaging path.
Let not your beauty lie
In needing beauty's praise.
Only let it, bye and bye.
Be naught to what stays.
In this fair time
See the enduring grace
More sublime
Than what time will erase.
Disdain that beauty, all so brief,
And look to another day's pleasure
When what is lost to time's thief
Will be replaced by love's greater treasure.

TO FIND STRENGTH

Amidst great love
We face harsh realities
That test that love.
But we find beauty and harmony
In what nature has provided
And what strength and heart has given
To overcome.

TO OVERCOME
(for Dawn D'earth)

One cold wintry night
I curled up next to the fireplace
With its crackling fire
That led me into drowsy thoughts
Of things that made me sad.
The sadness heightened
As I thought of Dawn and her strength and courage
In her fight against the ravages of cancer.
And I thought of John at her side
Unyielding in his fight, too,
A bastion that adds to her battle
To overcome.
And as I saw the shadows from the fire fade,
My eyelids grew heavy for a peaceful sleep,
Knowing that whatever else happens
Love will triumph with hope to keep.

A TOUCH OF HEAVEN
(to Judy)

We took a chance on all-embracing love
And went to the summit
Where we touched heaven,
Whose light was our beacon of joy.

There we could see out special world
Stretched out before us,
A splendid magic land
For us to command.

As we gave ourselves to each other
Our hearts overflowed with love,
Where dwells our treasure troves
To give each other immeasurable riches.

Each touch, each kiss, each embrace,
Each loving word to hold and retrace
And each soaring thrill that seized us,
Made each moment so very precious.

After the fullness from each climaxing crescendo
There came that delicious calm
With your face bathed in a radiant glow
And our soft words spoken as beautiful as a psalm.

Remember all things done in shining, pristine love,
And gently come as on the wings of a dove,
In the quest for vibrant fulfillment,
Enriches the body and mind, from heaven sent.

This was our "first time"
And carried us to the sublime;
Its memory will not perish
And will remain for all time to cherish.

TRUE BELIEVER

You are not a true book lover
or a dedicated collector
If you don't have books
Overloading your capacity
With many books standing on the shelves
In front of others
And others lying flat
Strung out along each shelf
To stack more and more.
Each nook and corner is not overlooked
Waiting for more to join them
That only passion can explain.

UNFAIR TREATMENT

There is a female clan
Whose object is to please any man.
It's known as the oldest profession
To satisfy the male's sexual obsession.
And when they get caught practicing their art
They go to the slammer while their clients freely depart.

UNHINGED

As true poets,
We must write about ourselves
As the representatives of the miseries
Caused by a broken world
And of the internal terror
That haunts us in countless ways,
Hopelessly.
If we as poets feel the agonies ourselves
We can't ignore them
In their depth of pain and despair.
There is no relief,
And they are with us every day,
Every hour of the day,
Every minute of the day,
Even every second of the day
As the news consumes us,
In countless ways:
Economic distress,
Loss of jobs,
Loss of homes,
Loss of businesses,
Drugs,
Family stress,
Loss of faith,
Loss of values,
Hurricanes,
Wars and their consequences,
Ad infinitum.
We cannot escape the hurt
Worldwide beyond our control.
It all engulfs us
At every turn.
And it all makes us wonder:
Were we born to suffer?

A VALENTINE OUT OF SEASON

A lovely blond may delight my eye
Or a fetching figure may get a hi,
Or an affluent lady may fill my need
And appeal to my tempting greed.
The ladies come in all shapes and sizes
And just to look at some the libido rises.
But surely you rise above them all
And have saved me from my licentious fall.
Your beauty, talent, charm and fun,
Those and more make you the only one,
Would you be my eternal Valentine?

WALL FALLEN

While riding through Virginia's rolling hills,
I came upon a long stone wall in disarray,
And if meant for the ages,
It was poorly laid.

Rising from the land of many stone walls,
This shambled wall seemed out of place
And would never be mended
In this place where beauty reigns.

The wall assuredly once graced the land
Erected by a farmer's calloused hands
And made from the randomly scattered stone
Conveniently native to the land.

Was the wall made to confine roaming cows
Or made to go nowhere
For beauty rather than functional use
Because the stone was there?

I could see the wall was beyond repair
And lies there scarring the land.
If the builder was still around
He would sadly see his wall had fallen.

WEEPING WILLOW

Weeping, weeping is the willow
Weeping in all it's glory,
Mighty in height,
Lush and heavy laden,
Yet lithe at the bending of the limbs,
And though the limbs hang heavily down,
Not to heaven bent,
It looks comfortable with itself.
So don't weep for the weeping willow,
It need not look to heaven,
For God's hand in its making was
Not to make it carry
A heavy burden,
But to give beauty.
Which gives life to a splendid thought--
Could the tree be kneeling,
Bent in prayer?

WE'LL MEET AGAIN

The brush
Guided by an inspired hand
Captured our moment as on a canvas
In all the lights and shadows
Joy and pain
Anticipation and excitement.
The brush is not dry
And the hand, poised,
Will paint again.

WHERE IS MY FATHER?

Where is my father
When my life is at stake?
Who is my friend
When I'm about to be executed?
Who will plead my case
When my mother condemns me
And an apostle of Hippocrates
Betrays his oath?
They choose not to hear my silent cries,
And she will never see my baby smiles.
She will never see me grow
Through my failures and successes
And through my tears and laughter,
Always comforting and praising me.
She will not give me a chance
To make the dean's list
Or look beautiful for the prom.
She will not give me the chance
To be a doctor or lawyer or executive
Or a mother
Or even president.
How can I comfort her someday
When she would need me,
For me to comfort her?
How can I have the chance
Never to sentence to death
An innocent baby in my womb?
No, all will be finished quickly for me,
Dirty, messy, bloody,
Ignominiously disposed of,
Like garbage.
Where is my father?

WHERE SOLACE IS FOUND

In the silence of a reclusive life,
Sealed from the passions that sustain the heart,
I search for solace in desperate ways
Because the one I love is beyond my reach
And I see her in such fleeting time
That hastens me back to my desolate chamber
Where dwell my dreams and fantasies of her.
As the days and nights pass in vain,
Visions of her fall into lines like these that bear
The long hours of pain because she's not there.
And that is where the solace is found,
Because in writing lines where she can live in the mind
I can make beautiful images of her abound.

WHOSE TRUTH?

What is truth?
It's a question that takes you
Into a slippery realm
Of answers put forth with passion,
Often fiercely fought,
Even among giants of intellect,
Claiming their truth is the truth.
Then let the subject slide into
The burning subject of whose religion
Holds the truth
And you'll see passion rise in flames
Into a deadly, consuming game.
The depth of feeling has left a long path
Of hate and vitriol
In continuing shame,
Whether Protestant, Catholic,
Muslim, or Jew
And whatever holy group you can name
They all go to their holy books
And vigorously claim,
It was all done in God's name.
And their truth lies there,
Which makes us wonder:
While only God makes the truth
Why did we not get a clear message from him,
That would not give room for contentiousness
Or equivocation.

THE WONDER OF BEING

A single blade of grass
Seems unimportant,
Yet the whole world
Depends on it as proof
That it is a miracle of life
So small yet so vital
That it would come
Only from the hand of God.
How powerful this small thing of life
That it matters it requires sun and water
To thrive.
It deepens the mystery
That the best minds of science can't explain
And solve such a small thing,
And more so the great wonder of being
And how it all began.

WRITER'S ADVICE

If you want to write a gripping story,
One proven way is to make it gory.
But if you want to titillate instead,
Don't delay, get the characters in bed.

YOU ARE THE POEM

God is the poet,
And you are the poem—
In the beauty of your face,
In the music of your voice,
In the rhythm of your walk,
In the depth of your emotions.
You are the poem,
Not these feeble words.

YOUR GIFT

When I give to you,
I am enriched more than you.
When you accept it,
I know you are accepting me.
Your presence is your gift to me,
And you fill all the space I need—
I can then never be lonely.

YOUR PRESENCE

In the gloomy nights of piercing grief
There was little or nothing
That gave hope, balm, or relief.
Then your presence,
Your smiles, your sweet voice,
Your touches, your embraces,
Your hugs, your kisses, our conversations,
Full of passionate delights
To transform all around me
The seeming deathliness of a mortuary
To the comfort and vibrancy of a sanctuary.
All this renewed from a lovely past,
A beautiful friendship now recast,
Can light the future with loving abundance;
Surely it all rests on your vibrant presence.

II. HAIKU

1.

A rotting fence
left standing in solitude
memories of youth.

2.

The steaming desert
rises up all around you
and follows you.

3.

Snow scenes in August
Christmas cards
ordered early.

4.

An empty church
all prayers overheard there
echo in silence.

5.

Footsteps
in my dead mother's bedroom
no one there.

6.

Baby's death
mother mourns
with breasts full of milk.

7.

Empty pond
too dry to weep
for missing frogs.

8.

The winter rain
beating against the windows
the smell of vegetable soup.

9.

Tears flowing down the cheeks
are they from sadness
or from happiness.

10.

Two faces
smiling
during a whisper.

11.

A dark alley
dead end
to homeless.

12.

The frog
jumped into the pond—
kerplunk.

13.

Out of the thick woods
a hulking, roving bear
is smelling the daisies.

14.

The sound of children
scrambling to the Christmas tree
for Santa's largess.

15.

Riders on the bus
late at night
all faces blank.

16.

Laugh or cry
the sun
rises and sets.

17.

A hot in the woods
feathers drifting to the ground
a sudden silence.

18.

A family of deer
find a banquet
among the azaleas.

19.

A fresh uniform
packed for an extended trip
with tears all around.

20.

Red, red roses
in full bloom—
artificial.

21.

Hidden
off the edge of the piano
crickets sing their song.

22.

Full moon
resting
in a placid pond.

23.

From his cage
a staring orangutan
follows a butterfly.

24.

In the falling snow
a solitary figure
mourns at a new grave.

25.

The school bell
opening up
a whole new world.

26.

Zoo elephant
standing like a statue
listening for jungle sounds.

27.

Snow flake by snow flake
the landscape is transformed
overnight.

28.

The swans on the lake
moving effortlessly
nonchalant.

29.

Sunny day
in the park
full of debris.

30.

Gentle breeze
field of daisies
ballet dancers.

31.

Power lines
rest stop
for birds flying south.

32.

Hunters wait
a deathly blast
a deer falls.

33.

Evergreens
preening themselves
in winter winds.

34.

Daffodils
unkempt
after a storm.

35.

Freshly fallen snow
blemished
by footsteps.

36.

The moonlight
through the rustling leaves
trembles on the ground.

37.

An aborted baby
doesn't cry—
forever.

38.

A child's funeral
many mourn
teddy bear waits at home.

39.

The full moon
kept its promise
lovers embrace.

40.

Stately Douglas firs
steady against the wind
ready for Christmas.

41.

The ancient castle
perched on the distant hill
carved out of mist.

42.

The mountain in the distance
keeps drawing closer and closer
seeming never to arrive.

43.

The abandoned house
ready for the bulldozer
a hidden bird nest.

44.

Picking wild blackberries
for a pie
none left on return home.

45.

At the end
of the rainbow
no treasure.

46.

Stalled in the desert
the moon and the stars
my only companions.

47.

Terminally ill dog
pleading eyes
at the end.

48.

Empty swing
moving in the breeze
a child's funeral.

49.

Midnight
silence
except for the clock.

50.

A faded picture
yet radiant
with mother's smile.

51.

Orchard
heavy with fruit
full moon.

52.

Wildflower
reaching for the sunlight
in a sidewalk crack.

53.

The play of light
on the ceiling,
a view from the bed.

54.

The welcoming of the morning
in the early light—
contemplating the day.

55.

In the woods beyond
we hear the song of birds
but we can't see them.

56.

The squirrels and deer
flee from their wooded haven
being cleared for houses.

57.

A shaft of sunlight
reveals many surprised
in a darkened room.

58.

The blue sky
lost its reflection
on a dry lake.

59.

Twinkling fireflies
make a starry sky
among the phlox.

60.

Specks of lights
blinking in the summer night—
fireflies.

61.

A pattern of light
over the bed
a summer morning.

62.

A soft summer breeze
rustles the window curtains—
air conditioner on hold.

63.

Freshly fallen snow
blemished
by footsteps.

64.

Full moon
clear as day—
almost.

III. LIMERICKS

1.

There is a lady named Judy
Who is classy but never snooty.
She came on the scene
To be my bride and queen;
She's as sweet as tutti fruitti.

2.

There is a president named Clinton
Of him many girls were smitten
Along comes a sweet young thing
That resulted in a fling;
The rest of the story is forbidden.

3.

There is a Rick of geology
Who is also a student of theology.
He mows down politicians
When he sees skullduggery their mission
And does so without apology.

4.

Sally always plays the lottery,
Even though she lived on the edge of poverty.
One day she hit the jackpot,
Then squandered all she got.
Now Sally's back on the edge of poverty.

5.

TO MARY AND DAN
ON THEIR GOLDEN DAY

There was a Dan who went to war
Learning many things, therefore.
He fought in France
A place known for romance
And heard much about l'amour toujour.

And after he came home I'm here to tell,
He fell under that l'amour spell.
And who was it who did disarm
This former warrior with her special charm—
Her name was Mary, a southern belle.

Then daring Dan got very bold,
And whatever he said, it sold.
Mary was pleased she caught this Dan Juan,
The one she put her money on,
That has led to this day of shining gold.

It's important to note square dancing here
Because there Dan spread so much cheer.
You see many ladies came early to dance
To line up for their chance
To dance with this dashing cavalier.

And there is Mary with her southern charm,
Along with those virtues from the farm.
So if you want anything done,
Look no further, she's the one;
You won't need to twist her arm.

And so we're all blessed with Mary and Dan
Who have the great gift of elan.
They have made their golden way
And together have glowed each day;
Surely their marriage was made in heaven.

www.ingramcontent.com/pod-product-compliance
Lightning Source LLC
Chambersburg PA
CBHW072007040426
42447CB00009B/1530